KELLY SLATER

EXTREME SPORTS STARS

BY MATT SCHEFF

SportsZone

An Imprint of Abdo Publishing
www.abdopublishing.com

www.abdopublishing.com

Published by Abdo Publishing, a division of ABDO, PO Box 398166,
Minneapolis, Minnesota 55439. Copyright © 2015 by Abdo
Consulting Group, Inc. International copyrights reserved in
all countries. No part of this book may be reproduced in
any form without written permission from the publisher.
SportsZone™ is a trademark and logo of Abdo Publishing.

Printed in the United States of America,
North Mankato, Minnesota
042014
092014

Cover Photos: Marco Garcia/AP Images, right,
Victor R. Caivano/AP Images, left
Interior Photos: Association of Surfing Professionals/
AP Images, 1, 24-25; Jeff Flindt/NewSport/Corbis,
4-5; Joli/A-Frame/Zuma/Corbis, 6-7; Zuma Press/
Icon SMI, 8-9, 26, 27, 28-29; Christopher Halloran/
Shutterstock Images, 10, 30 (right); Rui Ferreira/
Shutterstock Images, 11, 15 (inset); Stan Liu/Icon
SMI, 12-13; Shutterstock Images, 14-15; Ricardo
Arduengo/AP Images, 16-17; Sean Davey/Aurora
Photos/Corbis, 18-19; Ben Margot/AP Images, 19
(inset), 30 (left); Pedro Monteiro/Shutterstock
Images, 20-21; Reed Saxon/AP Images, 22-23, 31

Editor: Chrös McDougall
Series Designer: Maggie Villaume

Library of Congress Control Number: 2014933914

Cataloging-in-Publication Data
Scheff, Matt.
 Kelly Slater / Matt Scheff.
   p. cm. -- (Extreme sports stars)
Includes index.
ISBN 978-1-62403-458-9
1. Slater, Kelly, 1972- --Juvenile literature. 2. Surfers--United
States--Biography--Juvenile literature.   I. Title.
797.32092--dc23
[B]
                                              2014933914

CONTENTS

PERFECTION

It was an ideal day for surfing at the Billabong Pro Tahiti surfing competition in 2005. The world's top surfers were carving up 6-foot (1.8-meter) waves as they battled for one of the world's biggest surfing titles. Two men were fighting it out in the final surf: Kelly Slater and Damien Hobgood.

Kelly surfs in 2005 in Indonesia.

Kelly rides under a huge wave in 2005 in Hawaii.

FAST FACT

Kelly broke his own record for the highest two-wave score in history. He'd earned a 19.93 in the same event in 2004.

Kelly had already gotten a perfect score of 10 on one of his early waves. But each surfer would be scored on his two best waves. So Kelly once again dropped in. His board hung on the back of the wave as it curled over him, creating a barrel. Kelly's surfing was flawless. The judges gave him another 10, for a perfect total of 20! No surfer had ever done that before. Kelly was the champion.

*Kelly rides at the
2013 US Open of Surfing.*

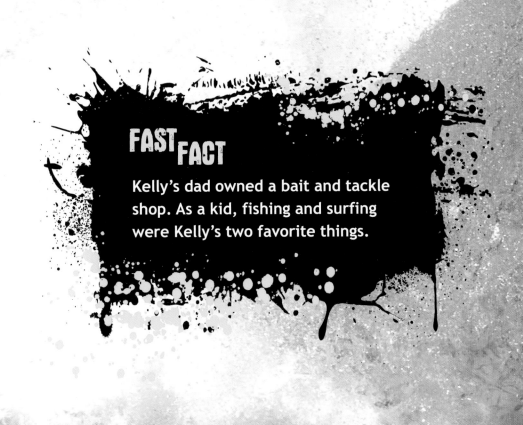

EARLY WAVES

Robert Kelly Slater was born February 11, 1972, in Cocoa Beach, Florida. Florida isn't known for great surfing. The waves are slow and gentle. That didn't stop Kelly. At just five years old, he grabbed a bodyboard and caught his first wave. Soon, he was standing on the board, surfing. He

Kelly competes in a
2012 event in California.

Kelly was a natural on the waves. He entered his first competition in 1980, at age eight. But he didn't even have a real surfboard. He had to ride on his bodyboard. It didn't seem to matter. Kelly pulled off a series of 360s (full spins) and won his age group.

Kelly celebrates a win at a 2010 event.

Soon, Kelly had a real surfboard, and his natural skill was turning heads. He went on to win four national amateur championships. But life wasn't perfect. Kelly's parents divorced when he was 11. He and his older brother, Sean, lived with their mother.

Kelly battles with a wave during a 2012 competition.

Kelly gets huge air on a wave in 2013 in France.

FAST FACT

Fans started calling Slater "King Kelly" because of his long reign as world champion.

Surfing fans quickly learned that Kelly was a special talent.

KING KELLY

Kelly's reputation grew and grew. By the time he decided to turn pro in 1990, he was already one of the most famous surfers in the United States. Surfing companies begged him to use their gear. Fans turned out to see whether Kelly lived up to the hype. He did. In 1992, Kelly became the youngest man ever to win the world title. He was just 20

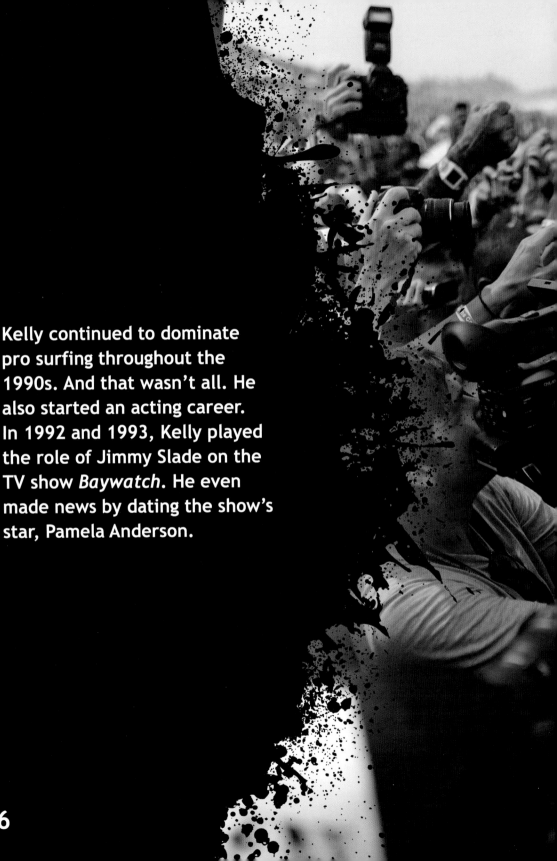

Kelly continued to dominate pro surfing throughout the 1990s. And that wasn't all. He also started an acting career. In 1992 and 1993, Kelly played the role of Jimmy Slade on the TV show *Baywatch*. He even made news by dating the show's star, Pamela Anderson.

Kelly's surfing abilities helped him become famous.

FAST FACT

Growing up, Kelly wanted to be a comedy actor. One of his favorite actors was Steve Martin.

*Kelly surfs in 1996
in Hawaii.*

18

From 1994 to 1998, Kelly won five straight world titles. He was breaking new ground. His control of the board allowed him to do more advanced tricks than anyone had ever done before. This sparked what surfers called the "new-school revolution," and it changed surfing forever.

Kelly rides a wave in 1997 in Hawaii.

Kelly shocked fans when he walked away from the sport in 1998.

FAST FACT

In 1998, Kelly and fellow surfers Rob Machado and Peter King formed a band called the Surfers. They released an album and even went on tour.

GONE AND BACK AGAIN

Kelly was the biggest star in the sport in 1998. Then he shocked the surfing world when he announced he would retire after the season. He said he was burned out. Kelly still surfed in a few events each year. But Kelly didn't compete for the world title for the next three years.

FAST FACT

Kelly worked with video game maker Activision to create his own video game, *Kelly Slater's Pro Surfer*. It was released in 2002.

Kelly competes at the 2004 X Games.

Kelly returned to the world tour in 2002. He finished just ninth that year. But soon he was back on top. From 2005 to 2011, he won five more titles. That gave him a total of 11. No other surfer in history has more than four.

Kelly shows off his surfing skills at the 2013 US Open of Surfing.

KELLY SLATER'S LEGACY

How long will Kelly Slater continue to compete as a pro surfer? Rumors about his retirement have swirled for years. But even into his 40s, Kelly is a contender every year to win another championship. But whenever Kelly does decide to hang up his surfboard, he'll do it as the greatest of all time.

Kelly competes at the 2013 US Open of Surfing.

Kelly rides a big wave at the 2013 US Open of Surfing.

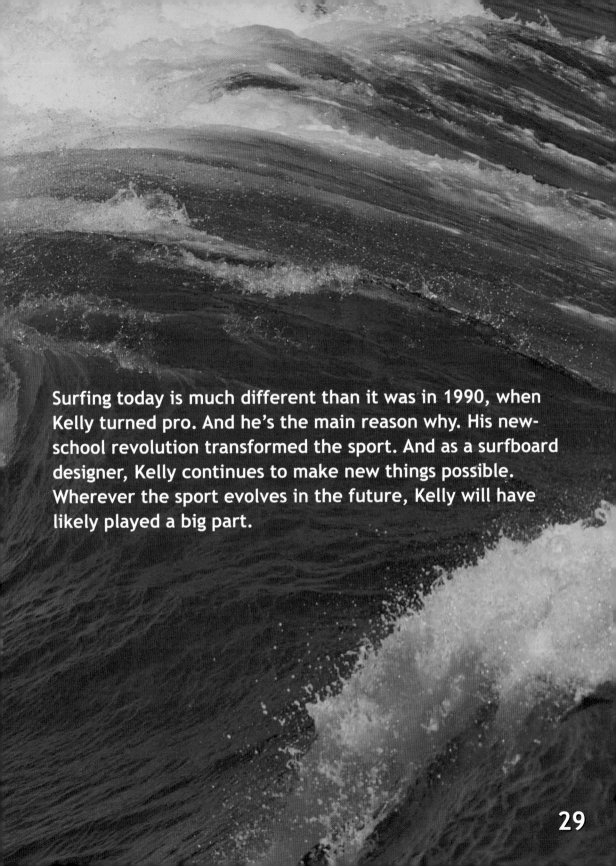

Surfing today is much different than it was in 1990, when Kelly turned pro. And he's the main reason why. His new-school revolution transformed the sport. And as a surfboard designer, Kelly continues to make new things possible. Wherever the sport evolves in the future, Kelly will have likely played a big part.

TIMELINE

1972

Robert Kelly Slater is born on February 11 in Cocoa Beach, Florida.

1980

At age eight, Kelly enters and wins his first surfing competition.

1990

Kelly begins to compete as a professional.

1992

At age 20, Kelly becomes the youngest world champion in surfing history.

1998

Kelly wins his fifth straight world title, then announces his retirement.

2002

Kelly comes out of retirement and rejoins the pro tour.

2005

At the Billabong Pro Tahiti, Kelly scores the first perfect-20 score in surfing history.

2011

Kelly wins his eleventh world title.

2013

At age 41, Kelly scores the second perfect-20 score of his career at the Volcom Fiji Pro.

GLOSSARY

amateur
A person who is not paid to compete in a sport.

barrel
The cylindrical shape a large wave makes as it crashes in toward shore; surfers ride inside the barrel.

bodyboard
A short, light board, similar to a surfboard, that people usually ride lying down.

contender
Somebody who could legitimately win.

new-school revolution
A movement in surfing during the 1990s during which surfers began performing riskier, more difficult tricks.

pro
Short for professional; a person who is paid to compete in a sport.

retire
To stop doing a job for a living.

360
A surfing trick in which a surfer and his board spin in a complete circle.

INDEX